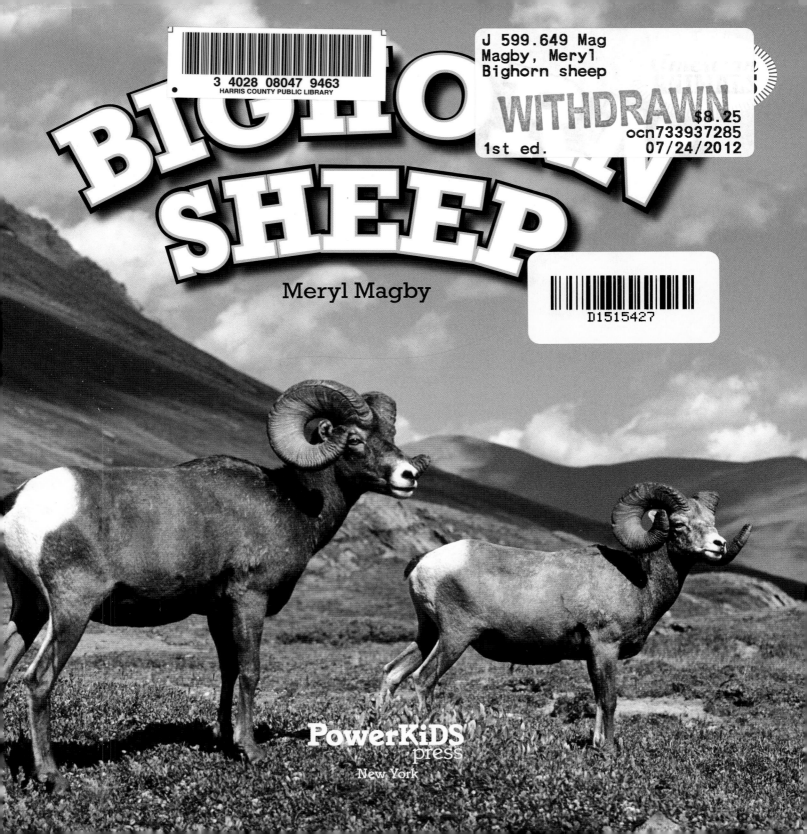

BIGHORN SHEEP

Meryl Magby

PowerKiDS press
New York

Published in 2012 by The Rosen Publishing Group, Inc.
29 East 21st Street, New York, NY 10010

First Edition

Editor: Amelie von Zumbusch
Book Design: Ashley Drago

Photo Credits: Cover © www.iStockphoto.com/Images in the Wild; pp. 4, 15 (bottom) iStockphoto/Thinkstock; p. 5 © www.iStockphoto.com/Rick Parsons; pp. 6, 7, 9 (top), 16–17, 19, 20, 21 Shutterstock.com; p. 8 © www.iStockphoto.com/Lisa Kyle Young; p. 9 (bottom) © www.iStockphoto.com/Steven Tulissi; p. 10 © www.iStockphoto.com/Frank Leung; p. 11 © www.iStockphoto.com/Ken Canning; pp. 12–13 Darrell Gulin/Getty Images; p. 14 Danita Delimont/Getty Images; p. 15 (top) Bob Bennett/Getty Images; p. 18 © www.iStockphoto.com/Jyeshern Cheng; p. 22 Greg Russell/Alpenglow Images/Getty Images.

Library of Congress Cataloging-in-Publication Data

Magby, Meryl.
 Bighorn sheep / by Meryl Magby. — 1st ed.
     p. cm. — (American animals)
 Includes index.
 ISBN 978-1-4488-6181-1 (library binding) — ISBN 978-1-4488-6321-1 (pbk.) — ISBN 978-1-4488-6322-8 (6-pack)
 1. Bighorn sheep—Juvenile literature. I. Title.
 QL737.U53M2237 2012
 599.649'7—dc23
                                2011026309

Manufactured in the United States of America

CPSIA Compliance Information: Batch #WW12PK: For Further Information contact Rosen Publishing, New York, New York at 1-800-237-9932

Contents

Mountain-Climbing Sheep

Did you know that some of the best mountain climbers in the United States are sheep? However, these mountain climbers are not the **domestic** sheep that you find on farms and ranches. They are wild animals called bighorn sheep.

Bighorn sheep live in the mountains and deserts in some parts of the American West. They

Male bighorn sheep, such as this one, have horns that are longer, thicker, and heavier than those of females.

Bighorn sheep have an excellent sense of balance. They can stand on ledges that are only 2 inches (5 cm) wide.

are named for the large, curved horns that male bighorn sheep have. These amazing animals have **adapted** to living at high **elevations** where very few other animals live. They can survive in both very hot weather and very cold weather.

Desert and Mountain Homes

This desert bighorn sheep is in Grand Canyon National Park, in Arizona. Desert bighorns have lived in the area that is now the park for tens of thousands of years.

There are three different kinds of bighorn sheep. Rocky Mountain bighorn sheep live in the Rocky Mountain range that runs through parts of the western United States. Desert bighorn sheep live in desert mountain ranges in California, Nevada, Arizona, New Mexico, Utah, Colorado, and Mexico. Sierra Nevada

bighorn sheep live only in the Sierra Nevada mountain range in California.

The **habitats** of bighorn sheep may be different depending on where they live. However, most sheep like to live in steep, rocky mountain areas where they are safe from **predators**. They must also live close to places where they can find food and water.

This is a Rocky Mountain bighorn sheep. Rocky Mountain bighorns are the most common kind of bighorn sheep.

Hooves and Horns

Bighorn sheep can easily cover 20 feet (6 m) in one jump.

Bighorn sheep have adapted to life in their mountain and desert habitats. One adaptation is their hooves, which are soft and **flexible** on the inside. This lets the sheep climb steep cliffs and make long jumps that other animals cannot make.

Both male and female bighorn sheep have horns. Male sheep, or **rams**, have long curved horns that grow in a **spiral**. Female sheep, or **ewes**, grow much shorter, straighter horns. Rocky Mountain bighorn rams can weigh more than 300 pounds (136 kg). Desert bighorn rams weigh about 200 pounds (91 kg). Ewes tend to be smaller than rams.

A Rocky Mountain bighorn ram's pairs of horns can weigh as much as 30 pounds (14 kilograms).

This is a bighorn ewe. Bighorn ewes and rams both have tan or brown coats with white patches on their nose, their rear, and the backs of their legs.

Finding Food and Water

Though Rocky Mountain bighorns like grass and grasslike plants best, they also eat shrubs.

Bighorn sheep are **herbivores**. This means that they eat only plants. In the Rocky Mountains, bighorn sheep eat grasses and grasslike plants in the summer. In the winter, they eat whatever plants they can find. Desert bighorn sheep eat green grasses and desert plants, such as cacti, for most of the year.

Bighorn sheep get a lot of water from the plants they eat. However, they also have to find places to drink water. During the hot summer months, bighorn sheep living in desert areas need to drink water at least every three days.

It is harder for many bighorn sheep to find food in the winter. This is because plants may die, lose their leaves, or get covered by snow.

Bighorn Sheep Facts

1. Bighorn sheep's special hooves let them move quickly on rocky ground. They can run 30 miles per hour (48 km/h) on flat ground and climb up steep slopes at 15 miles per hour (24 km/h).

2. Bighorn sheep have very good eyesight. This is important when they are jumping and climbing on rocky mountain slopes.

3. Bighorn sheep can see other animals, such as mountain lions, from about 1 mile (2 km) away.

4. In the desert, both male and female bighorn sheep use their horns to break open hard, prickly cacti. Cacti are a good source of both food and water for bighorns.

5. Bighorn sheep have stomachs that let them eat large amounts of food very quickly and rechew it again later so that they can **digest** it. This is called chewing cud.

6. Bighorn sheep that live in the Rocky Mountains grow thick coats with two layers of hair each winter. This helps them stay warm in windy, cold weather. They shed their winter coats in the spring.

7. Some bighorn sheep in California's Yosemite National Park wear special collars that let scientists know where they are. This helps scientists learn more about how sheep use their habitats.

8. Animals with antlers, such as deer, lose their antlers each year. Animals with horns, such as sheep, keep their horns for life. Each year the horns grow a bit bigger.

Rams, Ewes, and Lambs

In the summer, many Rocky Mountain bighorns head higher into the mountains to find food.

The bighorn sheep that live in the same area make up a **herd**. However, the sheep in a herd do not stay together all year long. The ewes in each herd tend to live in smaller groups, called bands, with their lambs. The rams in the herd form their own bands. For most of the year, the rams stay away from the ewes and lambs.

However, the two groups come together each fall during the **mating** season.

Bighorn sheep are always watching out for predators, such as mountain lions. They use their sharp eyesight, hearing, and sense of smell to tell if a predator is close.

A bighorn sheep's eyes are set wide apart and near the front of its head. This lets the sheep see a wide area easily.

Each band of ewes and lambs is lead by one ewe. This ewe is known as the dominant ewe.

15

Crashing Horns

The mating season for bighorn sheep comes each fall. At this time, rams fight each other by crashing their huge curved horns together. They do this to decide which rams get to mate with the ewes. Only the strongest rams that win the most fights will mate that year.

When animals hit their heads together, it is known as butting heads. Bighorn rams have been known to butt heads for as long as 20 hours in a row!

The rams charge at each other at about 40 miles per hour (64 km/h). Sometimes their horns get locked together as they fight. The tips of some rams' horns break from crashing together. The crashes of their horns can be heard from 1 mile (2 km) away.

Growing Up

Young bighorn lambs are white and fluffy. After a few months, they grow adult coats of fur.

Bighorn ewes most often have one lamb each year. Bighorn lambs can run and jump a few days after they are born. At first, lambs stay close to their mothers and drink their milk. After a few weeks, the lambs spend most of their time playing with other lambs.

Bighorn lambs drink their mothers' milk until they are between four and six months old.

Not all lambs make it through their first year. This is because there may not be enough food or water for the lambs to stay strong. Mountain lions also hunt lambs because they are not as fast as adult bighorn sheep. However, many bighorn rams live to be about 10 years old in the wild. Ewes live about 12 to 20 years.

Bighorns and People

Native Americans made this rock carving in what is now Utah's Canyonlands National Park. The animals on the bottom and right are bighorn sheep.

Before Europeans came to North America, there were millions of bighorn sheep living in the present-day United States. Many native peoples hunted bighorns for food. They also made bows from the sheep's horns. However, by 1900, there were only a few hundred bighorns left in the United States. They started

to die out because too many people were hunting them. They also caught **diseases** from the domestic sheep brought to North America by the Europeans.

Today, the number of bighorn sheep in the United States is still low. Sierra Nevada bighorn sheep are **endangered**. This means they are in danger of dying out.

By 1960, there were only about 17,000 bighorn sheep living in North America.

Bighorn Sheep Today

Today, scientists and government **agencies** are working to make sure the number of bighorn sheep in the United States keeps growing. They study the sheep, keep their habitats safe, and make sure that they do not catch diseases.

Some of the best places to see bighorn sheep today are national parks. Bighorn sheep live in several parks, including Colorado's Rocky Mountain National Park and Montana's Glacier National Park. If you visit one of these parks, you may see bighorn sheep on the ledges high above you!

These desert bighorn sheep are in Joshua Tree National Park, in California. About 250 bighorn sheep live there.

Glossary

adapted (uh-DAP-ted) Changed to fit requirements.

agencies (AY-jen-seez) Special departments of the government.

digest (dy-JEST) To break down food so that the body can use it.

diseases (dih-ZEEZ-ez) Illnesses or sicknesses.

domestic (duh-MES-tik) Having to do with animals that were raised by people.

elevations (eh-luh-VAY-shuns) The heights of objects.

endangered (in-DAYN-jerd) In danger of no longer existing.

ewes (YOOZ) Female sheep.

flexible (FLEK-sih-bul) Moving and bending in many ways.

habitats (HA-buh-tats) The kinds of land where an animal or a plant naturally lives.

herbivores (ER-buh-vorz) Animals that eat only plants.

herd (HURD) A group of the same kind of animals living together.

mating (MAY-ting) Coming together to make babies.

predators (PREH-duh-terz) Animals that kill other animals for food.

rams (RAMZ) Male sheep.

spiral (SPY-rul) Having a curved or curled shape.

Index

Web Sites

Due to the changing nature of Internet links, PowerKids Press
has developed an online list of Web sites related to the subject
of this book. This site is updated regularly. Please use this link to
access the list:
www.powerkidslinks.com/aman/sheep/